ISRAEL
REPAIRING THE WORLD

RABBI STEPHEN WISE

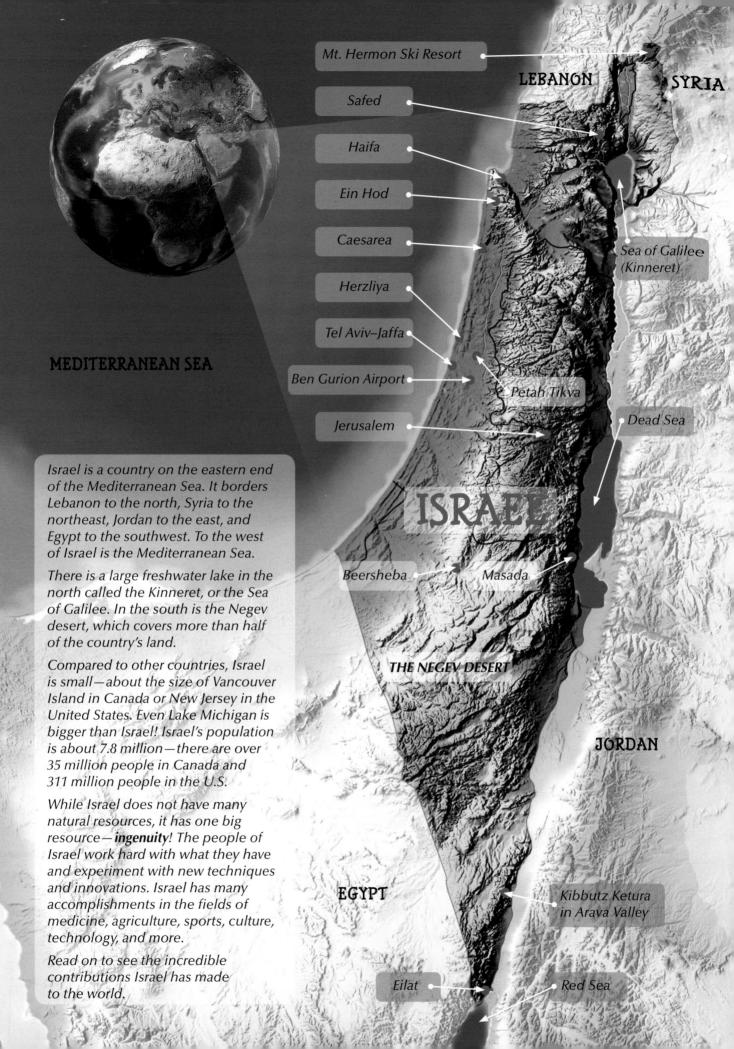

MEDITERRANEAN SEA

Mt. Hermon Ski Resort

LEBANON

SYRIA

Safed

Haifa

Ein Hod

Caesarea

Sea of Galilee
(Kinneret)

Herzliya

Tel Aviv–Jaffa

Ben Gurion Airport

Petah Tikva

Jerusalem

Dead Sea

ISRAEL

Israel is a country on the eastern end of the Mediterranean Sea. It borders Lebanon to the north, Syria to the northeast, Jordan to the east, and Egypt to the southwest. To the west of Israel is the Mediterranean Sea.

There is a large freshwater lake in the north called the Kinneret, or the Sea of Galilee. In the south is the Negev desert, which covers more than half of the country's land.

Compared to other countries, Israel is small—about the size of Vancouver Island in Canada or New Jersey in the United States. Even Lake Michigan is bigger than Israel! Israel's population is about 7.8 million—there are over 35 million people in Canada and 311 million people in the U.S.

While Israel does not have many natural resources, it has one big resource—**ingenuity**! The people of Israel work hard with what they have and experiment with new techniques and innovations. Israel has many accomplishments in the fields of medicine, agriculture, sports, culture, technology, and more.

Read on to see the incredible contributions Israel has made to the world.

Beersheba

Masada

THE NEGEV DESERT

JORDAN

EGYPT

Kibbutz Ketura
in Arava Valley

Eilat

Red Sea

CONTENTS

HISTORY OF THE LAND AND PEOPLE

The people of modern-day Israel share the same language, culture, and religion as their ancestors, who first lived there 3300 years ago. Groups of Jews have lived in Israel ever since. While the Jewish people also lived in other countries all around the world, they always hoped to **re-establish** a Jewish homeland in Israel, the land of their ancestors. In 1948, the Jewish community in Israel, under the leadership of David Ben-Gurion, were granted statehood by the United Nations. The modern State of Israel was declared on May 14, 1948.

THE PATRIARCHS AND MATRIARCHS

The people of Israel trace their origin to Abraham, who was the first person to believe in one God. Abraham and Sarah, their son Isaac and his wife Rebecca, and their grandson Jacob, along with Leah and Rachel, are the **patriarchs** and **matriarchs** of the Israelites. These families lived in the Land of Canaan, which came to be known as the Land of Israel.

JEWISH KINGS

The Jewish people were once ruled by kings. The greatest kings were King David (1010–970 BCE), and his son Solomon (970–931 BCE). King David made Jerusalem the capital of Israel and King Solomon built the First Temple there.

⍌ *The Temple was a national place of religious worship for the Jewish people.*

HOW ISRAEL GOT ITS NAME

✡ It is said in the Bible that the name Israel was given to the patriarch Jacob after he fought hand-to-hand with an angel. "*Isra-el*" means "one who has struggled and prevailed with God." Jacob's twelve sons gave origin to the Twelve Tribes of Israel that later formed the Jewish nation.

⍌ *Israeli postage stamp showing the emblems of the Twelve Tribes of Israel.*

CHANGE OF RULE

In 587 BCE, the Babylonian army captured Jerusalem and destroyed the First Temple. The Jewish people rebuilt the Second Temple but eventually lost their independence in the Land of Israel. Different empires have ruled or controlled Israel throughout history. In ancient times, Israel was part of the Babylonian, Persian, Greek, Roman, and Byzantine Empires. In the Middle Ages, Islamic and Christian crusaders fought over the land. And in modern times, Israel was part of the Ottoman Empire and the British Empire.

⌄ In ancient times, Roman armies conquered most of the known world.

THE HOLOCAUST

During World War II (1939–1945), the Nazi regime in Germany killed six million Jews in a deeply tragic event known as the Holocaust. The Nazi Holocaust proved again the need to re-establish the Jewish state to provide a safe home for Jews all around the world.

⌄ Present-day Israel is a modern country that leads the world in many ways.

OUT INTO THE WORLD

When the Romans conquered the Land of Israel in 70 CE, they destroyed the Second Temple. Most of the Jewish people were forced to leave the land. They travelled throughout the Middle East, Europe, and North Africa. Scattered outside of the Land of Israel, the Jewish people established rich cultural and economic lives. They **contributed** greatly to the societies where they lived. But they also maintained their national culture and prayed to return to the Land of Israel.

⌃ David Ben-Gurion declaring Israel's independence, under a portrait of Theodor Herzl.

MODERN ISRAEL

In the 19th century, **Theodor Herzl** organized the leaders of the Jewish world. They dreamt of returning to the land of Israel to form a modern state. After many struggles, Israel declared its independence on May 14, 1948. The United Nations recognized Israel as an independent state under international law.

➢ Statue of David Ben-Gurion.

EDUCATION ABOVE ALL

Following the tradition of past generations, education is very important in Israel. Education is the key to the future. The **graduates** of Israeli schools and universities are producing some of the most advanced technologies in the fields of computers, **telecommunication**, medicine, agriculture, and **biotechnology**.

ONLY IN ISRAEL

Israel is probably the only country in the world where **research institutes** and a university were established before it became an independent state.

THE OLDEST SCHOOLS ...

The Technion – Israel Institute of Technology is a public research university in the city of Haifa. Founded in 1912, Technion is the oldest university in Israel. The university offers degrees in science and engineering.

The Agricultural Experiment Station in Tel Aviv was founded in 1921, and later became the Agricultural Research Organization. It is Israel's main facility for research and development in the field of agriculture.

The Hebrew University of Jerusalem, founded in 1925, is now a world leader in medical research and health care.

⅄ *Opening ceremony of the Hebrew University of Jerusalem on April 1, 1925.*

PEOPLE OF THE BOOK

✡ The National Library of Israel has more than five million books. The library's mission is to store a copy of all material published in Israel in any language. The library also collects books on the subject of Israel, the Land of Israel, Judaism, and the Jewish people published in any language and in any country in the world.

⅄ *The Daniel Sieff Research Institute was established in 1934. It is now the Weizmann Institute of Science, one of the world's leading research centers.*

NOBEL PRIZE FOR ISRAEL

In 2004, Israeli chemists Aaron Ciechanover and Avram Hershko of the Technion won the Nobel Prize for chemistry. In 2009, Ada E. Yonath became the first Israeli woman to win the Nobel Prize, also in chemistry. In 2011 Dan Shechtman also won the Nobel Prize for chemistry.

In total, ten Israeli politicians, writers, **economists**, and scientists have received the Nobel Prize for their achievements.

➤ *The Nobel Prize is the world's most prestigious award. It was created by Swedish chemist Alfred Nobel in 1895. The prize is awarded in the fields of chemistry, economics, literature, medicine, physics, and peace.*

FAMOUS GOVERNORS

✡ The First Board of Governors of the Hebrew University of Jerusalem included **Martin Buber**, Albert Einstein, **Sigmund Freud**, and **Chaim Weizmann**.

⌄ *Albert Einstein is one of history's most famous scientists.*

... AND MANY NEW ONES.

There are many great universities in Israel, such as Tel Aviv University, the University of Haifa, and Ben-Gurion University of the Negev, with its main campus in Beersheba. All Israeli universities and colleges offer world-class education and training to thousands of students from Israel and around world.

⌄ *Students talking in front of one of the many buildings of Tel Aviv University. With almost 30,000 students, Tel Aviv University is Israel's largest university. It is also the largest Jewish university in the world.*

EDUCATION COUNTS

✡ Israel's workforce is among the most highly educated in the world. Over twenty percent of Israel's working population holds **academic degrees**.

HEALING THE WORLD

Israel is a world leader in medicine. Scientists and doctors in Israel are always experimenting and inventing new medical devices and treatments. Israeli know-how and innovations have made significant contributions to the field of medicine.

A CAMERA YOU CAN SWALLOW

Imagine swallowing a video camera the size of a pill! The PillCam was developed by the Israeli company Given Imaging. The PillCam is a smooth capsule that a patient can swallow. It has a miniature camera that takes over 50,000 images inside the body over an 8-hour period. Doctors use the images to help decide on the best treatment.

Doctors in more than 60 countries use the PillCam to take pictures of the **digestive tract**. The PillCam has helped more than 122,000 patients worldwide.

⋎ *There are many hospitals in Israel committed to healing patients and to medical research. Soroka Medical Center is the major medical center in the Negev. It is responsible for the care of over a million people, including 400,000 children. Soroka treats a diverse population of Jews, Ethiopians,* ***Bedouins****, and Arabs. Soroka doctors and scientists are involved in genetics research that helps people in Israel and all over the world.*

↖ *The PillCam capsule has its own source of light.*

↖ *Doctor reviewing the images taken by the PillCam capsule.*

GREAT HEALTHCARE

✡ All citizens of Israel receive world-class health care. The Israeli health care system is universal, which means it is open to everyone and paid for by the government.

A ROBOT THAT PERFORMS SPINE SURGERY

World robotics expert Dr. Moshe Shoham of the Technion – Israel Institute of Technology invented the world's only robotic tool for back surgery. The SpineAssist is the only surgical robot designed to operate on the spine. The device may soon be used for brain surgery!

The SpineAssist device is very **precise** and reduces the time needed for surgery.

Developed by the Israeli company Mazor Robotics, the SpineAssist is used in many hospitals around the world, including the United States, the Netherlands, Germany, Russia, Switzerland, and Israel.

TOP DRUGS

✡ Israelis developed two of the three most common drugs used to treat Multiple Sclerosis (MS). About 70 percent of MS patients worldwide take an Israeli-invented drug.

⬈ Surgeons performing a spine surgery.

SMART HOSPITAL BED

The Israeli company EarlySense has created a new kind of health monitoring device that looks like a heating pad. The device is placed under a mattress, where it monitors heart rate, breathing, and body movements.

"Smart beds" with EarlySense technology are used in hospitals and nursing homes around the world. Nurses and caretakers use this technology to watch their patients more closely. This improves patients' health and makes hospital stays shorter.

⬊ The EarlySense device sends information to caretakers and nurses, allowing them to take better care of their patients.

9

ISRAELI MEDICINE BEYOND BORDERS

Israel is recognized in the world as a leading source of knowledge and innovation in the field of on-the-ground medicine.

ISRAELI BANDAGE

The Emergency Bandage was invented by an Israeli military medic, Bernard Bar-Natan. This bandage was the first major innovation of its kind in over 50 years! The **Emergency** Bandage is used to treat many types of wounds, even in the most extreme conditions.

The sterile bandage applies pressure to the injury. It is easy to wrap around the wound and it stays in place. The bandage can also be used as a **tourniquet** in cases of severe bleeding. The Emergency Bandage is nicknamed the "Israeli bandage" by American soldiers, who use it in the field. The bandage is so easy to use that even an injured person can apply it with only one hand.

⋏ The Emergency Bandage was first used for saving lives during **peacekeeping operations** in Europe.

⌄ U.S. troops practice the proper way to use the Israeli bandage.

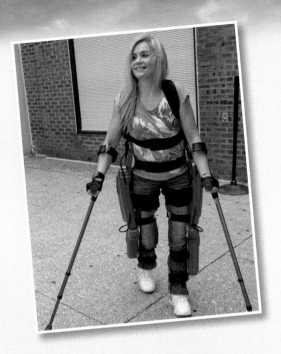

STAND UP AND WALK AGAIN!

ReWalk was developed in Israel by Argo Medical Technologies. ReWalk helps people who use wheelchairs to stand, walk, and climb stairs. It is a light brace support suit that people can wear over their clothes. It has **motion sensors** and small motors. The ReWalk suit is run by a computer system that helps the legs to move.

◄ *The ReWalk suit improves the quality of life and physical health of its users in many countries.*

MR. MOSQUITO FIGHTS MALARIA

Dr. Yoel Margalith is the Director of the Center for Biological Control at Israel's Ben-Gurion University. He is known in many countries as Mr. Mosquito, and there is a good reason why.

Dr. Margalith discovered a bacteria called *Bacillus thuringiensis israelensis* (Bti). Bti kills mosquitoes and black flies. This reduces the spread of diseases caused by mosquito bites, especially malaria. Unlike chemical insecticides, using Bti doesn't cause any harm to the environment.

MOSQUITO AWARD!

✡ In 2003, Israeli scientist Yoel Margalith received the world's premier award in environmental science for his contribution to the worldwide fight against malaria.

⅄ *Since Bti was used along the Yangtze river in China, malarial infections caused by mosquito bites have dropped by 90 percent. Bti is also used to prevent river blindness in eleven African countries, saving the eyesight of thousands of people.*

COMPUTER TECHNOLOGY

Every day, all over the world, people's lives are made better by **hi-tech** Israeli products. Many computer components were invented and developed in Israel. There are many companies in Israel that do hi-tech work. In fact, only the **Silicon Valley** in the United States has more hi-tech companies than Israel. Israeli engineers and technology professionals are hard at work making our daily lives better through hi-tech products and computer components.

COMPUTING IN ISRAEL

Your computer probably has components that were designed in Israel. There are hundreds of Israeli and international hi-tech companies in Silicon Wadi, including IBM, Google, Cisco, and Motorola.

Intel and Microsoft built their first overseas research and development centers in Israel. Israeli companies are very good at developing computer security and anti-virus technology. Checkpoint, an Israeli company, pioneered Internet and network security technologies such as the firewall.

✔ Most of the technology for the Microsoft Windows NT and XP operating systems was developed at the Microsoft facility in Israel.

SILICON WADI

✡ "Silicon Wadi" is a nickname for the coastal plain of Israel where there are many hi-tech companies. Silicon Wadi is named after the hi-tech "Silicon Valley" in California.

✔ Many hi-tech companies have their offices in Haifa.

12

GOING FOR THE BEST CHIPS

The most popular computer chip technologies, such as the Pentium 4 and dual-core processors, were designed at Intel's research centers in Israel.

And it gets even better. Intel's revolutionary Sandy Bridge microprocessor was also developed in Israel. It is faster and stronger than anything Intel has invented before. Sandy Bridge processors are used in laptops, desktops, cell phones, and tablets all over the world.

◀ *The new chip is a source of pride for Israeli engineers. It was developed at Intel's research facility in Haifa.*

⋏ *Intel building in the city of Petah Tikva.*

I SEEK YOU - ICQ

ICQ was the first instant messaging computer program. It was created by the Israeli company Mirabilis in 1996.

In the late 1990s more and more people were using the Internet. ICQ gave people a way to connect with other users in real time—instant messaging.

The American company AOL bought Mirabilis and its ICQ program for $407 million. At the time, this was the highest price ever paid to purchase Israeli technology.

AOL used the technology to develop its popular instant messaging system AIM. That was the beginning of what we use today to connect with people over the Internet.

➤ *With over 100 million users, ICQ is now available for all Mac, Windows and Linux computer operating systems as well as mobile web-based chatting for iPhone, Android, Symbian, and Blackberry devices.*

13

CONNECTING PEOPLE

Israel is a world leader in **communication** technology that connects people around the world. Over the years, Israeli companies have introduced innovations that have changed the way we live and connect with each other.

CELL PHONES EVERYWHERE

Motorola was one of the first global companies to open a research center in Israel.

Since 1964, Motorola headquarters in Tel Aviv has played an important role in some major mobile communication breakthroughs, such as the world's first car phone. In 2011, Motorola moved their headquarters to a modern building in Airport City near Ben Gurion Airport.

LEAVE A MESSAGE!

These days, everyone leaves messages over the phone. The Israeli company Comverse developed the first voicemail system.

In 1986, Comverse engineers first combined voice, fax, and calling functions into a single system. Today Comverse leads the world's messaging market.

⋏ The new Motorola building in Airport City is one of the largest buildings in Israel's hi-tech industry. It is an environmentally friendly "green building." The building has 30 laboratories, a library, and comfortable offices for the employees.

⋎ People in many countries use Comverse voicemail technologies with their phones and cell phones. With Comverse Visual Voicemail, they can choose to have all messages shown at the same time. They can also select any message in any order with one click.

HELPING THE BLIND

Project RAY, invented in Israel, developed a series of cellphone **apps** for blind people. RAY will help blind people around the world to become more independent.

The apps can help blind people to find their destination while walking down the street. They can also help make sure that users take the right medication when needed. Another app will make it easier to order and listen to audiobooks.

➤ *Smartphone apps can help blind people be more independent.*

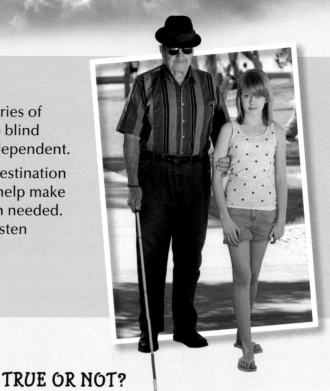

TAKING PICTURES WITH YOUR CELL PHONE

We all take pictures with our cell phones. Did you know it was an Israeli company called TransChip that made it possible?

TransChip developed the first **high-resolution camera** to fit on a single electronic chip for use in cellular phones.

▼ *Everybody likes to take pictures with their cell phones!*

TRUE OR NOT?

The Israeli company Nemesysco has developed a technology that can tell us if someone is telling the truth when talking on the phone. Nemesysco makes lie detectors and other products that are based on **voice analysis**.

The technology is used in airports in Israel and Russia, and by insurance companies and government agencies in the United Kingdom.

▼ *El Al is the national airline of Israel. Thanks to Israeli technologies, El Al has the world's best security when it comes to protecting passengers and flights.*

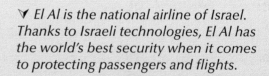

ISRAEL IN SPACE

The history of Israel in space is short, but quite impressive. It started in 1988 with the launch of Israel's own **satellite**. Israel has since made important contributions in a number of areas of space research. In June 2003, Israel was accepted into the European Space Agency (ESA).

JOINING THE SPACE CLUB

On September 19, 1988, Israel officially entered the space age by launching its own satellite with the Israeli-made Shavit launch vehicle. With that launch, Israel joined an exclusive club of countries like Russia, the United States, England, Japan, India, France and China, that have developed, produced, and launched their own satellites.

▼ *Satellites have many different functions. Weather satellites observe changes in the weather and climate of the Earth. This image shows a hurricane as seen from space.*

SMALL BUT MIGHTY

✡ Israel launched a micro-satellite into orbit in June 1998. This satellite is a marvel of miniaturization. It was developed at the Technion in Haifa. The satellite is an 18-inch (46 cm) cube that weighs only 106 pounds (48 kg). The micro-satellite orbits 516 miles (830 km) above the Earth, generating its own energy from the Sun. The micro-satellite takes pictures of the Earth using miniature cameras and computers.

▼ *An image of the eastern Mediterranean region and Israel taken by a satellite camera.*

EXPLORING MARS

NASA's mission to Mars was possible thanks to Israeli scientists. Mathematical calculations developed at the Technion in Haifa were very useful on Mars! These calculations allowed the Opportunity and Spirit rovers to run on **solar** power and send pictures back to Earth.

Both rovers have made important discoveries about the environment on Mars. They have found signs suggesting that there was water, and possibly a form of life, on Mars in the distant past.

⤏ The Spirit rover is a robotic vehicle designed to explore the planet Mars. The Rover landed on Mars on January 4, 2004.

◄ Planet Mars at sunrise

ISRAELI ASTRONAUT

In January of 2003, NASA launched the 28th flight of the **space shuttle** Columbia. The seven crewmembers on board included the first Israeli **astronaut**, Ilan Ramon.

The 16-day mission was devoted to research and included over 80 experiments in earth and space sciences. Israeli schoolchildren were able to communicate with Ramon during his flight. The entire country was proud of their first astronaut.

Sadly, on February 1, 2003, the space shuttle Columbia broke apart when re-entering the Earth's **atmosphere**, and the seven astronauts were killed. Despite this terrible tragedy, Israel continues to cooperate with NASA and the ESA to explore new boundaries of science and honor the sacrifice of the astronauts killed aboard the Columbia.

⤏ Ilan Ramon, the first Israeli astronaut.

MAKING THE DESERT BLOOM

Israeli scientists and farmers have always worked together on improving **agricultural yields** and quality. Israel's experience with desert farming and limited freshwater supplies helps people in dry regions around the world.

GROWING PLANTS – DRIP BY DRIP

One of the most important innovations in farming is the Israeli invention of drip **irrigation**. In drip irrigation, plastic pipes with small holes are laid on the ground. The holes release a controlled amount of water near the roots of plants. Each plant gets just the right amount of water to help it grow. This method saves a lot of water. Even **brackish water** can be safely used to water plants this way.

FISHING IN A DESERT

Can you imagine how this is possible? Israeli scientists have found a way to raise fish in the desert. They realized that brackish water drilled from underground desert reservoirs hundreds of feet deep could be used to raise warm-water fish.

Many fish farms have been built in the Negev desert. The fish is eaten by people in Israel and exported to other countries.

⋎ *Tilapia is the most common fish species raised in Israel's fish farms.*

⋏ *The holes in irrigation pipes are called "drippers." Drippers can be installed at any distance to fit the needs of any crop.*

⋎ *Israel's fish farming methods are used to feed people around the world.*

FLOWERS FOR ALL

✡ Flowers are Israel's leading agricultural export. Flower farms in Israel grow a wide variety of flowers. These include cut flowers such as roses, carnations, gerbera, and "summer flowers" from Europe.

▼ Grown in the warm regions of Israel, flowers are exported to Europe during the winter season.

COWS AND COMPUTERS

For several years, Israel has held the world record for milk production. Israeli dairy cows produce more than enough milk for all of Israel. The extra butterfat is used to produce a wide variety of dairy products. All the cows in Israel are a special breed called Israel-Holsteins. This breed is **resistant to disease** and can cope with Israel's hot climate.

▼ Computers are used to manage the feeding and milking of the dairy cows in Israel. Israeli dairy equipment and experience are used worldwide.

GREAT ISRAELI TOMATOES

Israeli tomato growing expertise has become legendary. The cherry tomato was developed in Israel. So was the Antonella, a tomato that keeps its firmness and flavor even after a week at room temperature.

Israel recently developed a tomato strain called Intense that doesn't drip and make your salad soggy. The liquid stays in, no matter how the tomato is cut or sliced. Intense tomatoes are great for making sandwiches and fancy salads.

➤ You can bite into an Intense tomato, just like you would bite into an apple, and the juice will not dribble down your chin.

POWER FROM THE DESERT

Israel is a very sunny land with very little rainfall. Israeli scientists understand the **potential** of generating power from the sun. They have also found ways of supplying the land with drinkable water by removing salt from seawater. Israel's new technologies promise an even brighter future for the entire world.

DESERT FLOWER SUN STATIONS

The Israeli company AORA started generating solar power in Israel in 2009. The AORA Tulip Tower uses mirrors called heliostats to reflect sunlight onto a "bulb" at the top of the tower. Concentrated heat from the mirrors causes the air inside the bulb to heat to very high temperatures. That ultra-hot air is then piped to a **turbine** to generate electricity.

Tulip's revolutionary concept allows the system to operate in any weather, even at night. At night, when there's no sunlight, the system can generate electricity using fuels such as natural gas or diesel. Tulip Tower can even run in hybrid mode on cloudy days – sunlight and fuel work together to generate full power.

In 2012, AORA launched Europe's first air turbine solar power station in Almeria, Spain.

SUNNY ISRAEL

✡ The most promising source of electricity is the power of the Sun. The sun shines in the Middle East at least 330 days a year. Israeli scientists have invented many different ways to turn **solar energy** into electricity.

⛛ *Israel is a world leader in the use of solar hot water systems. Ninety percent of homes in Israel have solar-powered water heaters on their roofs.*

➤ *The AORA solar tower was designed as a flower in a desert, to symbolize harmony and balance with nature.*

FLOATING SUN STATIONS

Using energy from the Sun often requires solar panels that take up lots of land. Israel's Solaris Synergy has designed solar energy **grids** that can float on water. The grid is constructed of lightweight plastic and fiberglass. It can float on any freshwater, saltwater, or wastewater surface.

ISRAEL LEADS THE WAY IN MAKING SALT WATER SWEET

Having very little rainfall but plenty of seawater led Israelis to explore ways of turning salt water into drinking water. This process is called desalination. Desalination removes salts and minerals from salt water.

More than two thirds of the world is covered in water, but more than 90 percent of it is salt water. Israel has developed desalination solutions that are changing the world. Besides watering its own agricultural industry, Israel manufactured China's largest desalination plant and smaller ones on Caribbean islands. Many countries find themselves in need of desalination solutions, and Israel is there to help.

⊼ *This solar-on-water system also works as a water reservoir cover that helps reduce evaporation and protects the water source.*

⊼ *The president of Arava Power, Yosef Abramowitz (standing second left) and a group of Negev desert Bedouin leaders visit Israel's first solar field, Ketura Sun.*

SOLAR FIELDS IN NEGEV

Arava Power is an Israeli company that builds **solar fields** in the Negev desert. Lots of sunshine and unused land make the desert a perfect place for generating solar power. The company also works with the nomadic Bedouin tribes who live in the Negev. The solar fields built on their lands are bringing prosperity and new opportunities to Bedouin communities.

◁ *Israel's first solar field, located at* **Kibbutz** *Ketura in Israel's Arava Valley.*

TAKING CARE OF THE ENVIRONMENT

Since biblical times, the people of Israel have been committed to nature conservation. There are many programs in Israel today that work to protect the natural environment. From pre-school to university, environmental education is a top priority in Israel.

LEADING THE WORLD IN WATER RECYCLING

As the world's leader in water **recycling**, Israel recycles 75 percent of its waste water and **sewage**. It recycles much more water than any other country in the world. Spain, in a distant second place, recycles only 12 percent of its water.

Israel has several top-quality sewage treatment plants. Once the water is treated, it can be used for agricultural purposes, or returned to natural water sources.

PLANTING TREES

Israel is one of only two countries in the world that began the 21st century with more trees than it had in the previous century. Israel does not have many natural forests—its forests are all hand-planted.

An organization called the Jewish National Fund (JNF) works with Jewish people all over the world to make planting new trees in Israel possible. Since it was established in 1901, the JNF has planted more than 240 million trees all over the country.

⋏ As of 2010, 100 percent of the sewage from the Tel Aviv metropolitan area is treated. It is reused for watering fields and public parks.

⋎ The Jewish National Fund works hard to organize tree planting in Israel. Hand-planted green trees cover more than 250,000 acres.

BETTER PLACE FOR CLEANER AIR

✡ Israel formed a partnership with Better Place, making Israel the first country in the world to build an all-electric car transport system. It is a revolutionary system that should make Israel oil independent by 2020.

Better Place is a company that builds networks of electric cars, charging stations, and battery switch stations. Electric cars are not powered by gasoline, they run on electric power stored in the car's battery. Electric cars are called "zero **emission**" cars because they do not create emissions from burning gasoline. Such cars help protect the environment by reducing the pollution in the air.

Better Place builds charging stations and battery switch stations all over Israel, where electric cars can recharge their batteries or replace them with new ones. Batteries are replaced by a robotic arm. It takes about five minutes – less time than filling up a gas tank.

↖ *Better Place battery switch stations make everything possible. Now electric cars have the freedom to go anywhere in Israel, at any time, without ever running out of fuel. The model of the cars used with this system is the Renault Fluence Z.E. (for Zero Emission), a four-door sedan that looks like any other car.*

PROTECTING THE WILDLIFE

The Israel Nature and Parks Authority (INPA) is in charge of protecting nature and public land in Israel. Israel has over 190 **nature reserves** and more than 65 national parks. Together they make up almost 20 percent of Israel's land.

The INPA protects the wild animals that live in Israel and also works to protect **endangered species** such as vultures and the spotted leopard.

↘ *The INPA also re-introduces animals to the wild. Onagers (a type of donkey), ostriches, and Arabian oryxes (a type of antelope) were successfully re-introduced to the wilderness.*

WASTELAND INTO WONDERLAND

Ariel Sharon Park is an example of how an environmental hazard can become a national treasure.

The Hiriya landfill between Ramat Gan and Tel Aviv was once the country's largest dumping ground. It was closed in 1998 and is now being transformed into an ecological wonderland, the Ariel Sharon Park.

The park will include an amphitheater, restaurants and cafés, sports fields, and educational sites to teach about society and the environment. The park will be three times the size of New York City's Central Park.

RICH ISRAELI CULTURE

Israel's rich culture comes from its worldly population—immigrants from all continents of the world with diverse ethnic subcultures. This mix of cultural and religious traditions, with a variety of skills and talents, has created the Israeli culture, which is dynamic and diverse.

MUSIC AND ART

When it comes to entertainment, Israel has a lot to offer. Israeli dance companies, such as Batsheva and Bat Dor are well known in the dance world. Theater in Israel is also diverse, with productions in Hebrew, Yiddish, French, Arabic, Russian, **Ladino**, and English. Habima, the national theater, was established in 1917. There are also regional theater companies throughout the country.

Israel has its own Philharmonic Orchestra, founded even before the State of Israel was created. Almost every city in Israel has its own orchestra.

There are major art museums in Tel Aviv, Herzliya, and Jerusalem and artist colonies in Safed, Jaffa, and Ein Hod.

FAMOUS ORCHESTRA

✡ The Israel Philharmonic Orchestra (IPO) is the leading symphony orchestra in Israel. It is one of the best orchestras in the world. Every year, the IPO tours the world's cultural centers and celebrated music festivals. The IPO also plays at special concerts throughout Israel as part of the "Arts for the People" project and at concerts for Israeli soldiers at their outposts.

The orchestra's first concert took place in Tel Aviv on December 26, 1936. The concert was conducted by the great Arturo Toscanini.

▼ The Israel Philharmonic Orchestra performing at Royal Albert Hall in London, England.

CHAGALL'S MASTERPIECE IN GLASS

The Abbell Synagogue at the Hadassah University Medical Center in Jerusalem is well-known for its beautiful stained glass windows. Marc Chagall, the famous Jewish artist, created the set of twelve huge windows in 1962. They are based on biblical motifs with each window representing one of the Twelve Tribes of Israel. Many visitors and tourists visit the synagogue every year to admire the beatuy of Chagall's masterpiece.

➤ *Artist Marc Chagall (left) at the dedication ceremony of his stained glass windows at Hadassah University Medical Center.*

THE MACCABIAH GAMES

✡ Many great Israeli athletes have won medals in international competitions such as the Olympic Games. And since 1932, Israel has hosted its own version of the Olympics every four years—the Maccabiah Games.

⌄ *Over 7000 Jewish athletes from around the world competed in the 2009 Maccabiah Games. Even more athletes are expected in 2013.*

⌄ *Entrance to the courtyard of Ralli Museum in Caesarea, Israel.*

SPORTS NATION

The people of Israel love sports. Basketball and soccer are very popular. Israelis have competed in many international competitions, including the Olympic Games. The Maccabi Tel Aviv basketball team has repeatedly won the European League Title. Windsurfing and water skiing are also popular, especially since windsurfer Gal Fridman won Israel's first and only Olympic gold medal in 2004.

Israel's beaches provide great opportunities for sports too. Israelis love to play a beach paddleball game called *matkot* in Hebrew. Players keep the ball in the air by hitting it from paddle to paddle. Israel also has the highest **per capita** number of qualified **scuba divers** in the world.

GREAT MUSEUMS

Israel has the largest number of museums per capita in the world. There are over 200 museums in Israel. They are treasure houses of archaeology, religion, local history, and art. Millions of visitors tour Israeli museums every year.

TOURISM IN ISRAEL

Visitors to Israel can see some of the world's most important historical sites. There are amazing beach resorts in the south and mountain climbing and skiing in the north. Tourists can travel back in time at 3000-year-old archaelogical ruins in central Israel. Travelling through Israel allows tourists to see the building of the modern State of Israel within this ancient land.

WONDERS OF THE WORLD

There are many important historical sites and monuments in Israel. Jerusalem, Israel's capital city, is home to the Western Wall, the Dome of the Rock, the Temple Mount, and the Church of the Holy Sepulchre. In southern Israel, visitors flock to the heights of Masada, the Dead Sea, and the Red Sea port town of Eilat. In northern Israel, tourists can walk through the ancient Roman ruins of Caesarea and the mystical cobblestone paths of Tzfat (Safed).

TOURING THROUGH NATURE

Israel is also a great place for hiking and visiting nature reserves. National parks in Israel have well-marked trails with beautiful views of wildlife and nature.

⋎ *When visiting Israel, find a friend to show you the many interesting sites, like this view of the Western Wall (right) and the golden Dome of the Rock (left) at sunset.*

MILLIONS OF TOURISTS

✡ About two million people visit Israel every year. Most of them are young travelers with their families.

⋎ *Tourists will find great hotels in Eilat and throughout Israel.*

SKIING IN ISRAEL

The average ski season at the Mount Hermon ski resort lasts only 45 days. But that's plenty of time to ski down the slopes and build a snowman! The Mount Hermon ski slopes are spread out across 31 miles (50 km) of hills on the northern border.

▽ Tourists from all over the world enjoy scuba diving in the Red Sea.

△ Ski lifts at Mount Hermon ski resort carry skiers to the top of the slopes. Besides skiing, visitors can have fun sledding and snowboarding.

FUN AT THE BEACHES

Israel has three seas, the Dead Sea, the Red Sea, and the Mediterranean Sea, as well as the freshwater lake known as the Sea of Galilee. All four offer beautiful beaches and great opportunities for swimming.

One of the most beautiful coral reefs in the world can be found in the waters of the Red Sea. The plentiful fish and coral formations have made it a world-famous diving site.

▽ The Dead Sea has deposits of black mud. The mud is easy to spread on the body and provides the skin with nourishing minerals.

SALTY SPA

The Dead Sea is a true national treasure. At 1368 feet (417 m) below sea level, it is the lowest point on Earth. It is called the Dead Sea because its water is so salty that nothing can live in it.

But that salt also provides great relief to the Sea's many visitors. People from all over the world come here to enjoy the healing qualities of the water. Many hotels, restaurants and shopping centers make a visit even more enjoyable.

REACHING OUT

Even though Israel is a small country, it has a long tradition of providing help to ease hunger, poverty, and disease in other countries. When **natural disasters** strike beyond its borders, Israel is always ready to respond. Government organizations like MASHAV and IsraAID provide help to people in need all over the world.

RESCUE TEAMS

Israeli rescue teams are always ready to respond when natural or man-made disasters happen. After the 2010 earthquake in Haiti, Israel's 200-strong relief team was the first on the scene. The team set up a field clinic where medical teams helped save thousands of lives and deliver babies too!

In March 2011, powerful earthquakes hit Japan. Israel was one of the first countries to send help. This help included a medical team and a fully equipped field hospital.

*⋏ The Israeli team sent to Haiti included many rescue experts from the **IDF Home Front Command**, which has experience saving victims from collapsed buildings.*

⋎ Field clinics are temporary hospitals where people get emergency treatments.

AIDING THE WORLD

IsraAID is a humanitarian organization based in Israel. Since its creation in 2001, IsraAID has organized aid programs all over the world. IsraAID has helped cyclone and tsunami victims in Asia. IsraAID also provides long term help programs for starving communities and war refugees in Africa.

⋎ The earthquakes that hit Japan in 2011 caused a lot of damage.

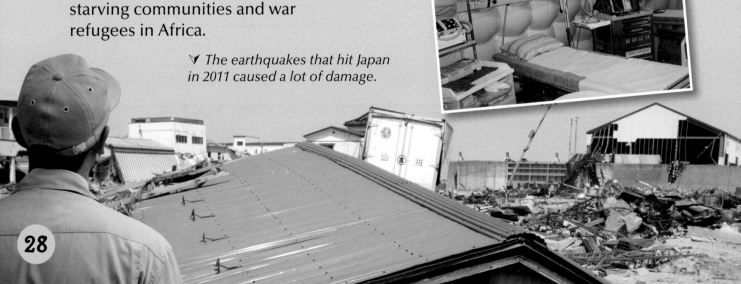

WELCOMING REFUGEES

Israel has been a safe haven for refugees from around the world. Since its creation, Israel has welcomed hundreds of thousands of Jewish people who were in danger, including almost one million from the former Soviet Union since 1989 (20 percent of Israel's population at the time).

Israel has also welcomed people of other religious and ethnic groups who are suffering or in need of a new home. In 2010 Israel welcomed a dozen refugees from ethnic fighting in **Kyrgyzstan**. In 2011 Israel rescued 40 children from **Eritrea** who were escaping the horrific regime that enslaved them into the army. In 2011 and 2012 a steady flow of hundreds from the war-torn Darfur region of Sudan in East Africa arrived and settled in Israel.

↖ *A young patient recovering after successful heart surgery.*

SAVING SICK KIDS

Since 1995, Israeli doctors and the Save a Child's Heart organization have given children from around the world free life-saving heart operations. Over 2,300 children have been treated since the organization first started.

JEWISH HEART FOR AFRICA

Jewish Heart for Africa is an organization that brings Israeli technologies to African villages. Its mission is to improve the lives of people in Africa with the help of Israeli innovations.

The organization installs Israeli solar panels and other technology to provide electrical power to schools, medical clinics, orphanages, and water pumping systems. Since the organization began in 2008, it has completed over 37 solar and agricultural projects. These projects provide light, clean water, food, and proper medical care to more than 150,000 people in Ethiopia, Tanzania, Malawi, and Uganda.

HELPING FARMERS

✡ Project Agro is a Jewish Heart for Africa program. It uses Israeli drip irrigation technology to help farmers grow more food.

▽ *Using drip irrigation technology helps grow more food with much less water.*

GLOSSARY

academic degree An award given by a college or university

agricultural yield The amount of crop grown on a field

apps An application or software, usually a game or special program, which you can dowload to your smartphone

astronaut A person trained to command, pilot, or serve as a crew member on a space vehicle

atmosphere A layer of gases surrounding the planet Earth

Bedouins Desert-dwelling people of North Africa and the Middle East

biotechnology A field of biology that uses living organisms in engineering, technology, and medicine

brackish water Water that contains more salt than fresh water, but not as much salt as seawater

Buber, Martin An Austrian-born Jewish philosopher and writer. One of the first professors at Hebrew University

communication The activity of sending and receiving information between two or more person

contribute To give or supply goods or services together with others

digestive tract A series of organs in a body that process food, starting with the mouth and ending with the anus

economist A professional in the field of economics

emergency A situation that poses an immediate risk to health, life, or the environment

emission A matter released into the air, such as fumes from a chimney or an automobile engine

endangered species Animals which are at risk of becoming extinct

environmental hazard Any situation that can pose a threat to the natural environment and make people ill

Eritrea A country in East Africa on the Red Sea

establish To bring into existence on a firm basis

Freud, Sigmund One of the world's most famous Jews and the father of modern psychoanalysis

graduate someone who has completed all required school courses and attained a degree

grid A frame made of crisscrossed parts

heritage Something inherited from the past

Herzl, Theodor The founder of modern day **Zionism**. Herz was born in France, convened the first World Zionist Conference in Basel in 1897, and was buried in Jerusalem on Mount Herzl, which was named after him.

high resolution camera A camera that takes high-quality pictures

hi-tech company A company that uses highly advanced technology or devices

IDF Home Front Command A unit of the Israel Defence Forces (Israel's army). Home Front Command specializes in the field of civilian protection, operating during emergency situations throughout Israel, as well as around the world.

ingenuity Inventive skill or imagination; cleverness.

irrigation Adding water to the soil in order to grow crops

kibbutz A communal settlement in Israel based on the principle of joint ownership of property

Kyrgyzstan A country located in Central Asia

Ladino A language of Sephardic Jews, based on Spanish with Hebrew elements and usually written in Hebrew characters

landfill A site where garbage is collected and buried

manuscript Hand-written letter, scroll, or book

matriarch A person regarded as the mother or founder of an order, tribe, or nation

monitoring system A system that observes a situation for any changes which may happen over time

motion sensor A device that responds to signals based on movements

NASA The National Aeronautics and Space Administration is the agency of the United States government that studies space and runs the space explorations

30

natural disaster Damage caused by natural causes such as floods, tornadoes, hurricanes, volcanic eruptions, or earthquakes

nature reserve An area where wildlife is protected

patriarch A person regarded as the father or founder of an order, tribe, or nation

peacekeeping operation The activity of keeping the peace by military forces

per capita A Latin term that translates into "by head." It means "average per person."

potential Possibility, opportunity

precise Accurate and exact

recycling A process of treating waste materials so that they can be used again

re-establish To establish again

research institute A place where research is done

resistant to disease Not likely to become sick or diseased

satellite An object which has been placed into Earth's orbit by humans

scuba diver Underwater diver that uses an oxygen tank to breathe

sewage The waste water from homes and businesses

Silicon Valley The southern part of the San Francisco Bay Area in California. The region is home to many of the world's largest computer technology corporations.

solar A term used to describe things relating to the Sun

solar energy Energy created by the light and heat from the Sun

solar field A field where solar energy is harnessed

solar station A commercial power plant that uses concentrated solar energy to create electricity

space shuttle A vehicle that carries astronauts to space and back

telecommunication Passing of information over long distances using technology

tourniquet Anything that is tied tightly around an arm or leg to control bleeding by stopping the flow of blood through its vessels

turbine A rotating engine that extracts energy from a flow of fluids or gases and converts it into useful work

voice analysis the study of speech sounds

Weizman, Chaim A Zionist leader, president of the Zionist Organization, and the first president of the State of Israel

Zionism A Jewish movement from the late 19th century. The movement called for the Jewish people to return to their ancestral homeland.

INDEX

Information on how to obtain copies of this book may be obtained from:

Website: www.ma-tovu.ca

E-mail: sales@blueappleworks.com

Author: Rabbi Stephen Wise

Publisher: Joshua Avramson

Content Editor: Cheryl Wise

Copyeditor: Rachel Stuckey

Cover/book design: Tibor Choleva

Photo research: Melissa McClellan

Proofreaders: Rachel Stuckey, Walter Jansen

Photographs and reproductions:

© Dreamstime.com: p 7 middle (Cda2008); p 7 bottom (Siopw); p 14 (Arnd Rockser); p 11 bottom girl (Paula27); p 25 bottom (Iuliia Kryzhevska); p 25 bottom people (Ron Chapple); p 28 bottom (Yoshiyuki Kaneko)

© istockphoto.com: p 8 top (Alan Crawford); p 13 middle (4kodiak); p 15 top (LeggNet); p 22 bottom people (Maica); p 27 top (boryak); p 29 3rd from top (bagi1998)

© Getty Images: p 25 top (David Rubinger)

© NASA: p 16 middle, p 17 top & bottom; p 16-17 background

© photographersdirect.com: p 18 bottom (Hagai Nativ/PhotoStock-Israel); p 24 (Lebrecht Music & Arts Photo Library)

© PhotoStock-Israel: p 8 bottom (Shay Levy); p 14 top (Chris Sommers); p 15 bottom (Shay Levy); p 25 middle (Moshe Torgovitsky);

© Shutterstock.com: Cover image (Sergej Khakimullin/Tibor Choleva); Title page: flag (david n madden); Star image (Boris Stroujko/Tibor Choleva); Map page: Planet Earth (leonello calvetti); map (AridOcean); map illustration (Tibor Choleva); p 4 top (Kenneth Graff); p 4 bottom (Khirman Vladimir); p 5 top left (imagestalk); p 5 bottom (Rasmus Holmboe Dahl); p 5 bottom right (Vitaliy Berkovych); p 7 bottom people (Lentolo); p 9 top (Apple's Eyes Studio); p 9 bottom (Alexander Raths); p 11 2nd from top (xjbxjhxm123); p 11 3rd from top (Geir Olav Lyngfjell); p 13 bottom (Dmitriy Shironosov); p 15 middle (Lisa F. Young); p 16 bottom (Neo Edmund); p 18 top (Arkady); p 18 bottom left (Opas Chotiphantawanon); p 19 top left (kavram); p 19 top right (Alexander Dvorak); p 19 bottom (Arkadiusz Komski); p 20 bottom background, p 22 bottom (Protasov A&N); p 22 top (Tom Davison); p 23 bottom, p 26 top (Gorshkov25); p 26 bottom (Joshua Haviv); p 26 bottom right (Zurijeta); p 27 middle (frantisekhojdysz); p 27 bottom (Ryan Rodrick Beiler); p 28 top (ChameleonsEye); p 28 middle (ermess); p 29 top (homeros); p 29, 2nd from top (Monkey Business Images); p 29 bottom (Pichugin Dmitry)

p 8 middle, Courtesy of Given Imaging Ltd; p 10 top, U.S. Army photo by Specialist Joseph Francis; p 10 bottom, U.S. Air Force photo by Staff Sgt. Erica J. Knight; p 11 top, Courtesy of Argo Medical Technologies; p 11 bottom, © Tibor Choleva; p 12 top, © Alexander Zaprudsky; p 20 top, © Sonja Stark; p 20 bottom, Courtesy of Aora; p 21 top, Courtesy of Solaris Synergy; p 21 middle & bottom, Courtesy of Arava Power Company; 23 top, Courtesy of Better Place;

Public Domain: p 5 top right; p 6 top; p 6 bottom; (Yoav Dothan); p 7 top; p 12 bottom (Mattes); p 13 top (Ori)

Printed in Canada. 1st edition.

1 2 3 4 5   16 15 14 13 12